ALBERT

EINSTEIN

and Relativity

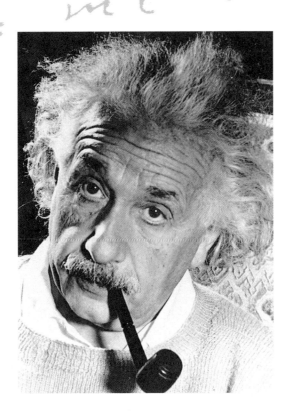

Steve Parker

Chelsea House Publishers
New York • Philadelphia

This edition © Chelsea House Publishers 1995

First published in Great Britain in 1994 by
Belitha Press Limited, 31 Newington Green,
London N16 9PU

Copyright © Belitha Press Ltd 1994

Text © Steve Parker 1994

Illustrations/photographs © in this format by
Belitha Press Limited 1994

1 3 5 7 9 8 6 4 2

ISBN 0-7910-3003-2

Printed in China for Imago

Acknowledgements

Photographic credits:
Archiv für Kunst und Geschicte, 6 Erich Lessing,
    8 top left, 9 top, 11 bottom, 12, 18 top, 20 top
    left, 23 top, 24 top
Bridgeman Art Library, 7 left Burghley House,
    Stamford , Lincolnshire
Camera Press, 22 bottom
Mary Evans Picture Library, 4 top
Roland Grant Archive, 20 top right
Hulton Deutsch Collection, 5 top, 16 top, 23
    bottom, 25 and inset, 29
Image Select, 4/5, 7 right, 8 top right and bottom,
    28 bottom
Popperfoto, 9 bottom, 24 bottom
Rex Features, titlepage
Science Photo Library, 10 top Lawrence Berkeley
    Laboratory, 11 top David Parker, 16 bottom
    Catherine Pouedras, 17 Tony Craddock, 18
    bottom ESA/PLI, 20 bottom NASA, 22 top US
    National Archives, 28 top and 27 Julian Baum
Cover montage images supplied by Mary Evans
Picture Library, Hulton Deutsch Collection,
Image Select, Popperfoto and Archiv für Kunst
und Geschicte

Illustrations by Tony Smith
Diagrams by Peter Bull

Editor: Phil Roxbee Cox
Design: Cooper Wilson Limited
Picture researcher: Juliet Duff
Specialist adviser: Perry Williams

STEVE PARKER has written more than 40 books
for children, including several volumes in the
Eyewitness series. He has a bachelor of science
degree in zoology and is a member of the
Zoological Society of London.

Contents

Introduction

As part of a survey, over 1,000 people were asked to name a famous scientist. More than half of them chose Albert Einstein, the mathematician and **physicist** whose most famous ideas were published between 1900 and 1920. Yet only ten of these people had any real knowledge of how Einstein brought such enormous changes to the world of science.

This is not unusual when discussing Einstein. Plenty of people have heard of him, but his work is very complicated and hard to understand. Many of his ideas are difficult to grasp because they are so different from what we see in daily life. For example, how can time slow down or even stop? A book such as this can only try to tackle the main ideas of Einstein's work and explain them in a straightforward way without using mathematics.

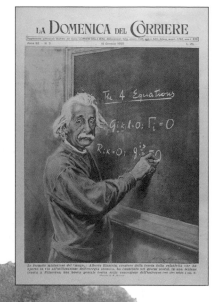

Einstein is pictured here on the cover of an Italian magazine in 1950. He is still one of the few scientists who are instantly recognizable around the world.

A view of Einstein's birthplace of Ulm, Germany, as seen across the River Danube.

Chapter One
The Early Years

Albert Einstein was born on March 14, 1879, in Ulm, in southern Germany. His mother, Pauline, and his father, Hermann Einstein, an electrical engineer, moved to the nearby city of Munich with Albert when he was just one. Hermann teamed up with his brother Jacob in a company making electrical instruments and equipment. Electrical engineering was big business in the late 19th century, but there were huge financial risks too.

Not an exceptional schoolboy

Young Albert was not outstanding at school. He was "slow and dreamy." At home, his uncle helped to develop his interest in mathematics. Albert was also fascinated by magnets and how they worked. His mother encouraged him in literature and music.

At the time, science was very popular in Germany. Many inventions, including the motorcycle and the car, were made by German pioneers.

Einstein with his younger sister, Maja, who was born in 1881. They enjoyed playing together.

Science at the turn of the century

At the end of the 19th century, there was enormous interest in the **physical sciences**.

1894 Italian inventor Guglielmo Marconi used radio waves for the first wireless transmission.

1895 German physicist Wilhelm Roentgen discovered X rays (X for unknown).

1896 French scientist Henri Becquerel detected natural **radioactivity** from uranium-containing chemicals.

1897 British physicist J. J. Thomson showed that particles existed that were smaller than **atoms**. They were later called **electrons**.

1898 J. J. Thomson confirmed that mysterious cathode rays, which had been studied for years, were streams of electrons.

1899 Ernest Rutherford (born in New Zealand) discovered two types of radioactivity, which he named alpha and beta rays.

1900 German physicist Max Planck introduced the idea that energy came in tiny "packets" which he called quanta.(see page 11).

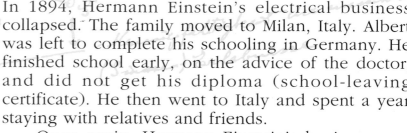

The scientific equipment used by Einstein during his studies at the ETH in Zurich, Switzerland.

On the move again

In 1894, Hermann Einstein's electrical business collapsed. The family moved to Milan, Italy. Albert was left to complete his schooling in Germany. He finished school early, on the advice of the doctor, and did not get his diploma (school-leaving certificate). He then went to Italy and spent a year staying with relatives and friends.

Once again, Hermann Einstein's business was unsuccessful. This time, his family went to Pavia, Italy, where the same thing happened. Albert's father wanted his son to become an engineer and start work, but Albert wanted to continue his studies.

The return of anti-Semitism

The Einstein family were officially Jewish. The 1880s saw the return of old prejudices, feelings, and actions against Jewish people. This is called anti-Semitism, and at the time, it was especially strong in Germany. Jewish people were blamed for problems, especially financial troubles. In the late 1890s, Einstein wanted to distance himself from Germany by becoming a Swiss citizen.

Back to school

Without a diploma, Einstein could not enter a university. However, the Swiss Federal Institute of Technology in Zurich (the famous ETH) accepted students if they passed an entrance exam. Albert failed it and went back to school, this time in Aarau, near Zurich.

He was taught by an inspiring physics teacher, August Tuschmid. A year later, Einstein went on to pass the ETH entrance exam and began his studies there in 1896.

At the Institute

At the ETH, Einstein did not show much interest in the lectures, but he did carry out some daring experiments. He tried to detect the invisible ether which was thought to carry light and other types of **electromagnetic waves** (see panel, right). Unfortunately, the experiment went wrong, and he only narrowly escaped serious injuries.

Einstein also studied the work of great physicists. Some 200 years previously, Sir Isaac Newton had devised theories and **equations** to explain the basics of matter, force, motion, and **gravity**. These had become the foundations of physical science.

Isaac Newton (1642–1727), whose views of the universe were overtaken by Einstein's.

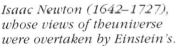

Waves and the ether

During the 19th century, scientists thought that electromagnetic waves had to travel in something in order to get from one place to another. They called this mysterious light-carrying substance luminiferous ether.

Scientists believed that all space, even between the stars, was filled by this substance. However, no one was ever able to detect it. Einstein's work finally did away with the idea of ether.

The new challenges

Since Newton, scientists had discovered forces and waves that he did not know about. Michael Faraday, André Ampère, and many others investigated electricity and magnetism. In the 1850s–1860s, Scottish physicist James Clerk Maxwell used mathematics to describe waves of electromagnetism and concluded that light was a particular type of electromagnetic wave. He suggested that there were other forms of waves, such as radio waves. A new scientific framework was needed, that could include these recent discoveries.

James Clerk Maxwell

Chapter Two
Molecules in Motion

In 1900, Einstein left the ETH in Zurich. He also became a Swiss citizen. He wanted to be a lecturer, but after doing odd teaching jobs, he ended up with a position at the Swiss Patent Office in Bern.

Einstein worked in the Patent Office from 1902 to 1909. Away from work, he continued his discussions with colleagues from the ETH, including Mileva Maric, a mathematician from Serbia. In 1903 he and Mileva married. They had two sons.

1905, a good year

Einstein carried out his scientific work mainly in his spare time. He lacked the benefits of someone in full-time research, such as long hours in lively discussion with scientific co-workers or reading the latest scientific journals. Yet in 1905, he had three very important articles published. The third article concerned the movements of tiny particles floating in a liquid or gas. This effect had been seen many years earlier by the Scottish plant expert Robert Brown. It was known as Brownian motion (see panel, below).

Einstein with his first wife Mileva, photographed in 1904. Mileva is holding their first son, Hans-Albert.

Brownian motion

Robert Brown (1773–1858) carried out many studies through the microscope. He also collected 4,000 types of plant on a trip to Australia.

In 1827, Brown looked at tiny grains of pollen through a microscope. Floating in water, the grains seemed to be knocked to and fro at random. These darting movements became known as Brownian motion, even though Brown himself did not know why they happened. It was to be Einstein who provided the answer.

Molecules and mathematics

Einstein took the ideas of the Kinetic Theory (see panel) and developed them further using mathematics. He worked out how particles of a certain size would react when hit by **molecules** of certain sizes, moving at various speeds. The Austrian physicist Ludwig Boltzmann had already carried out some of this work, as had American scientist Josiah Gibbs.

Another physicist working separately, Marian Smoluchowski, came up with results similar to Einstein's at around the same time.

Evidence for atoms and molecules

Einstein's calculations on Brownian motion were a great step forward. Many scientists saw them as evidence that things as tiny as atoms really did exist. Until then, ideas about atoms had been based mainly on speculations.

In 1908, French scientist Jean Perrin carried out careful studies of Brownian motion. He measured the movement of particles of tree resin floating in water and showed that Einstein's equations fitted the results. This was accepted as the first clear experimental evidence that atoms and molecules existed.

Kinetic Theory

At the end of the 19th century, ideas were developed about particles. In a solid, the particles were thought to move little in relation to each other. In a liquid or gas, however, the particles were thought to be always in motion, bouncing off each other and off the walls of the container. This was called the Kinetic Theory of Matter. At the time, scientists were unable to prove the theory.

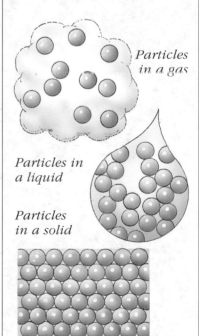

Particles in a gas

Particles in a liquid

Particles in a solid

Large scientific devices called bubble chambers were used to track the paths and collisions between tiny particles.

Electromagnetic waves

Electromagnetic waves have both electrical and magnetic energy. In the emptiness of space, they travel at the speed of light (see page 15). The waves can be measured in various ways.
• The wavelength is the distance from a point on one wave, such as the peak, to the same point on the next wave.
• The frequency is the number of waves passing a point in a certain time.
• So high-frequency waves are squashed together and have short wavelengths. The low-frequency ones are spaced out and have long wavelengths.

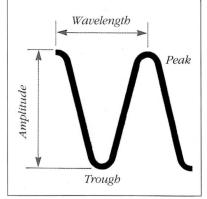

Chapter Three

Waves or Particles?

Another of Einstein's 1905 articles was about the energy from light turning into electrical energy. This happens when light hits certain metals. The energy in the light is passed on to particles in the metal called electrons. The electrons absorb the energy. As a result, they whizz out of the metal at high speed. If channelled along a wire, these electrons form an electric current. The change from light energy to electrical energy is called the photoelectric effect.

A long-running dispute

Scientists had been arguing about the nature of light for centuries. Some thought it was waves, others believed it was tiny particles. By the time of Einstein, the particle idea had been almost totally rejected.

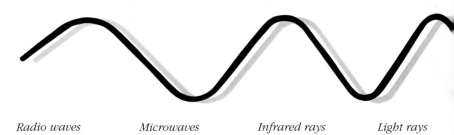

Radio waves   *Microwaves*   *Infrared rays*   *Light rays*

Scientists thought that the energy in light and other waves was continuous. That is, you could divide it into smaller parts, but you would never reach the ultimate, tiniest part.

Strange results

Many scientists, including J. J. Thomson, studied the photoelectric effect. They shone light (and other electromagnetic waves) onto metals, then measured the number and speed of the electrons given off. If light was a simple wave, then the brighter the light, the more energy it would have and the faster the electrons would whizz off. But this did not happen. The experiments showed that the speed of the electrons was linked to the **frequency** of the light.

Packets of energy

Einstein explained these results, adapting an idea introduced in 1900 by the German physicist Max Planck.

Planck had been working on an effect called black body radiation. A black body is an object that takes in all the energy falling onto it, including light energy, so it reflects no light. Planck managed to devise an explanation for the black body effect, stating that energy, such as light, was not continuous. Instead, the energy existed as tiny units or "packets," called quanta.

Electromagnetic waves change from long to short wavelengths.

Ultraviolet rays   *X rays*   *Gamma rays*

The colors of light

Different frequencies of light are different colors. In a **spectrum** or rainbow of light the red color at one end has a low frequency. The violet color at the other end has a high frequency.

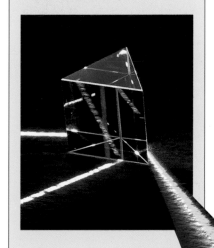

Einstein built on the work of Max Planck (1858–1947), the founder of quantum physics.

Light to electricity

This idea of energy packets, or quanta, went against the main beliefs of physics. But Einstein used it in 1905 to explain the photoelectric effect.

Imagine that a "packet of light energy" hits a piece of metal. This packet hits an electron and disappears, because the electron has taken its energy and moved away at high speed.

The speed of the electron depends on how much energy is in each packet of light. For example, packets of light energy from higher frequencies such as the color violet have more energy than those which are red – so the electrons they hit have more energy and go faster. It does not matter how bright the light is, because brightness comes from the number of packets of light arriving at a certain time.

A photograph of Albert Einstein taken in 1902 at the start of his career in the Swiss Patent Office, Bern.

The passing of classical physics

The work of Planck and Einstein quickly established the idea of quanta – not only in light but in many other forms of energy. The packet of light energy was thought of as a particle, known as the photon. Scientists could then treat light as waves for some purposes and as particles for others. This is called the wave-particle duality. It was a turning point in science. **quantum physics** was born.

Chapter Four

A Special Theory

In 1905, Einstein also published what became known as the special theory of relativity – "special" because it applies only under special conditions. The details of his reasoning and mathematics are extremely complicated. But the main idea of the theory and what it predicts can be explained in a simple way.

The scientist on the move

Imagine you are on a train. You roll a ball (in the direction you are traveling) and find its speed is two yards per second along the train's floor. The speed of the ball compared to you is, therefore, two yards per second.

A friend, watching from a station platform, can measure the speed of the ball through the window. It is rolling at two yards per second inside the train, and the train is passing at 50 yards per second through the station. So to your friend, the speed of your ball is 52 yards per second.

Who's moving?

You have probably experienced a simple version of the principle of relativity. You get into a train. It starts off very quietly and smoothly, and you don't notice you are moving. You only realize this when you see things going past the window. In effect, relative to the train, you are not moving.

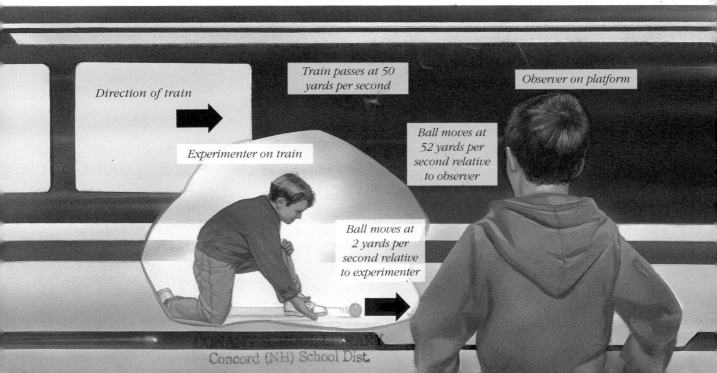

Direction of train

Train passes at 50 yards per second

Observer on platform

Experimenter on train

Ball moves at 52 yards per second relative to observer

Ball moves at 2 yards per second relative to experimenter

Relativity and light

One of Einstein's greatest insights was to apply the principle of relativity to light. Taking the mathematical equations of James Clerk Maxwell, he argued that the speed of light was the same for all observers no matter how fast they were going. So the speed of light is not relative. It is always the same (see opposite). It is shown as the letter c in scientific formulae because it is said to be the same, or **constant**.

Relative motion

So what is the real speed of the ball? Is it 2 or 52 yards per second? You might guess 52, because the station is not moving. But take the idea further. The station is on the surface of the Earth, which is zooming through space. To an observer deep in space, the Earth with the station is moving at over 30,000 yards per second!

This shows motion is not the same for everyone. It is compared to, or relative to, the observer. You cannot measure motion and speed unless you have something to compare it with.

The principle of relativity

This reasoning leads to the principle (not theory) of relativity, which has been around since the time of Galileo and Newton. It says that the laws of physics, including those of motion, are the same for all observers and objects who are moving at a constant speed and in straight lines relative to each other. In the example, both you and the train are going at the same speed, in the same direction. So you can think of yourself and the carriage as standing still.

Constant speed and traveling in a straight line are the 'special' conditions for the special theory of relativity. The general theory includes changing speeds and traveling in curves.

Extra distance

Back on the train, you have a very accurate light clock. It measures time by sending a flash of light from a bulb straight down to a mirror, which bounces the light back up to a sensor next to the bulb, which produces a tick.

You pass your friend on the station platform. Inside the train, you see the light going straight up and down. But what does your friend see? Each flash of light not only travels up and down but also travels sideways with the train. Your friend sees each flash form a **V** shape as the train zooms past.

The speed of light

When scientists talk about the speed of light, they usually mean its speed in the nothingness of space or a **vacuum.**

• Newton mistakenly believed that light took no time to get from one place to another. Its speed was infinite.

• The accepted most accurate measurement is 186,292.03 miles (299,792.458 kilometers) per second. So light could go round the Earth seven times in less than a second.

The light clock is used to explain the idea of time being relative. The experimenter on the train sees the light beam travel a shorter distance, compared to the observer on the platform. But the speed of light is the same for everyone. So time must vary.

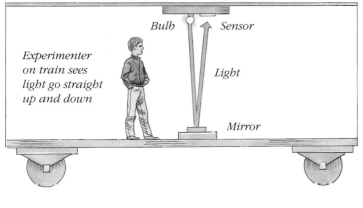

Experimenter on train sees light go straight up and down

Bulb Sensor Light Mirror

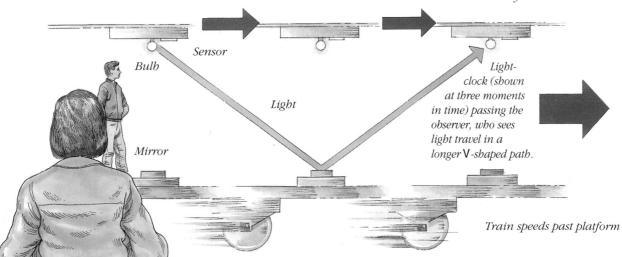

Sensor Bulb Light Mirror

Light-clock (shown at three moments in time) passing the observer, who sees light travel in a longer V-shaped path.

Train speeds past platform

Mass and energy

In Einstein's famous equation $E = mc^2$:
• E is energy.
• m is mass.
• c^2 (c squared) is the speed of light multiplied by itself – even in miles per second, a huge number!

This means a large amount of energy is equal to a tiny amount of mass, or matter. Tiny amounts of matter can be converted into huge amounts of energy. In **nuclear** power stations, the mass of radioactive fuels such as uranium and plutonium is converted into heat energy.

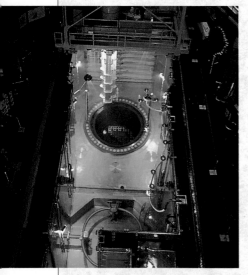

Fuel rods being loaded into a nuclear reactor, where their matter will change to energy.

A gathering of top scientists from around the world in Brussels in 1911. Einstein is standing second from the right, Planck is standing second from the left. Marie Curie, who invented the term "radioactivity," is leaning forward at the table.

Relative time

Here is the tricky bit. The speed of light is constant for all observers, however fast they are going. Speed is measured as distance per unit of time. So if your friend sees light travelling a longer distance, it must be taking more time. Therefore, each tick of the clock takes longer. To you, the clock is correct. To your friend on the platform, it is running slow. So we reach the conclusion that there is no such thing as universal, absolute time. Like motion, time is relative to the observer. The only constant is the speed of light, c.

A new framework for science

The ideas of absolute motion and absolute time were the basis of Newton's system of science. Einstein's theory and calculations finally did away with them. Einstein was greatly influenced by a book by the scientific thinker Ernst Mach. Mach had suggested that there could be no absolute motion or time.

The predictions of the special theory of relativity, described on the next page, seem very strange. But they only happen under extreme circumstances, when moving incredibly fast.

Weird happenings at high speeds

Special relativity predicts that, as an object approaches the speed of light:

• Time slows down. This is called time dilation. It was observed in 1941, in experiments on high-speed atomic particles called muons. It was also demonstrated in 1971, when extremely accurate clocks flew fast around the world on jet planes. After two days, the clocks had lost a fraction of a second compared to the same clocks on the Earth's surface because they had been moving faster.

• The object gets smaller. That is, it gets shorter in the direction it is travelling. If a space rocket could travel at half the speed of light, it would be about six-sevenths of its length on the launch pad. This effect had already been worked out in the 1890s.

• The mass of the object increases, so it gets heavier. This has been shown many times by experiments on fast-moving particles such as electrons. From this idea, Einstein developed his famous equation, $E = mc^2$ (see opposite).

Could you ever travel as fast as light? As your mass increased, so would the force needed to make you go even faster. At almost the speed of light, your mass would be so great that the force needed to give you that extra push would be impossibly huge. You would never quite get to the speed of light.

This observatory in Potsdam, Germany was named after Einstein. Scientists and astronomers use it to study space-time.

Chapter Five
Explaining the Universe

In the years following his articles of 1905, Einstein quickly became famous in the world of science. He received a PhD qualification, became a lecturer at the University of Berlin, then an associate professor of physics in Zurich. He moved on to become a professor of physics, first in Prague and then Zurich again. In 1913 Einstein took up the top position in Europe for a physicist – professor and director at the Kaiser Wilhelm Institute in Berlin. He held this post until 1933.

The special theory of relativity did not explain all Einstein hoped it would. From 1907, he tried to devise a more general theory, that would work for everything. The result was the general theory of relativity, completed in 1915 and published in 1916.

Like the special theory, the general theory is extremely complicated, but its main ideas can be explained in a simplified way.

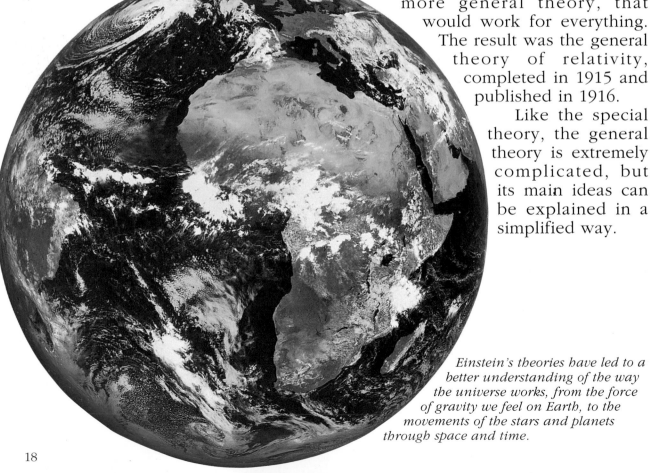

Einstein's theories have led to a better understanding of the way the universe works, from the force of gravity we feel on Earth, to the movements of the stars and planets through space and time.

On the move?

Before blast-off, an astronaut lies in a special seat in his space rocket. He is kept there by the force of the Earth's gravity. He feels it pulling him down as usual. The rocket takes off. As it gains speed, the acceleration presses him back into his seat. Once in space, the rocket settles down to a steady speed. The astronaut is weightless, floating around the rocket cabin.

He falls asleep and, on waking, finds himself pressed back into the seat. But why? There are two possibilities. One is that he has landed back on Earth and is feeling its gravity again. The other is that the rocket boosters have fired, pushing him into the seat as he accelerates to even greater speeds. He cannot distinguish between gravity and acceleration.

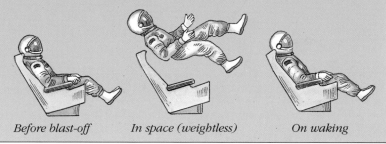

Before blast-off   *In space (weightless)*   *On waking*

The principle of equivalence

In 1907, Einstein realized that the force of gravity was equivalent to the force produced by acceleration. You cannot tell them apart (see the panel above). This is called the principle of equivalence.

This means there are two ways to measure the **mass** of an object. One is the force by which gravity pulls on it – the familiar "weight" here on Earth. The other is the force needed to make it accelerate. Today scientists use both. They are called gravitational mass and inertial mass, and they are equivalent.

Using the principle of equivalence, Einstein reasoned that the mass of a large object such as the Sun would attract the energy in something "weightless" like light. He was right.

The idea that time is relative has been used in stories for many years. One of the most famous is The Time Machine, *published in 1895 by H. G. Wells (far left).*

The pattern of radiation in space supports the idea that the universe began in an instant, known as the Big Bang.

Space and time

Other scientists had been working on the idea of special relativity. In 1908, the Russian-German mathematician Hermann Minkowski suggested that there are not three dimensions but four.

We are familiar with three dimensions of space (3-D, see panel, left). Minkowski's fourth dimension is time. Since this is so different from the usual way of thinking of time, it is very difficult to imagine or to draw pictures of it.

To work with the idea of four dimensions, Einstein used many ideas developed by other scientists. These include forms of geometry and maths pioneered by German mathematician Bernhard Riemann in the 1850s.

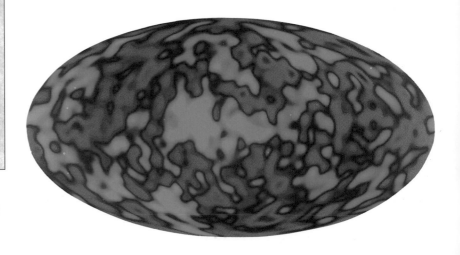

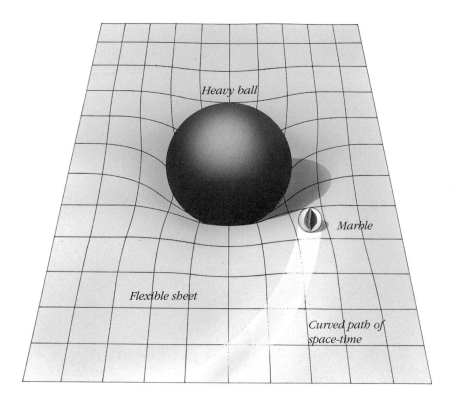

Heavy ball

Marble

Flexible sheet

Curved path of space-time

Passing every test

The general theory of relativity aimed to describe the workings of the universe more accurately than Newton's system of science. Einstein did this successfully.

However, general relativity did not have much practical use until the 1960s (see page 26). Then it became clear that it was an excellent explanation of space, time, motion, and gravity.

Space-time

Einstein and other scientists developed the idea of space-time – three dimensions in space and the fourth in time. Space-time is curved or bent by the mass of objects. The greater the mass, the more the bending. This bending represents gravity.

Imagine a flat rubber sheet with a square grid or "net" of lines on it. Roll a marble across the sheet and it moves straight along. This is like a space rocket passing through a region of smooth space-time.

Now put a large, heavy ball on the sheet. It bends the rubber and distorts the grid of lines. This large ball represents the huge mass of a planet, distorting space-time. Roll the marble now, and it goes down the slope to the planet. It follows the bend of space-time towards the mass, like a rocket pulled by a planet's gravity.

The idea of an expanding universe

Einstein's work showed that the universe should be expanding. At the time, it was thought to be still or static. So Einstein added a number called the cosmological constant to his equations to make them describe a static universe. Then the Soviet scientist Aleksandr Friedmann showed that the expanding universe was likely. Discoveries in astronomy by Edwin Hubble and others supported this view. The cosmological constant was not needed after all.

Chapter Six

Peace and War

After the publication of the general theory of relativity in 1916, Einstein realized that he had probably completed his greatest achievements. In 1921 he said "Discovery in the grand manner is for young people . . . and hence for me a thing of the past."

During the 1920s and 1930s, Einstein argued against the new quantum ideas in physics. These were being developed by Niels Bohr, with his model of the structure of the atom; Werner Heisenberg, with the **principle of uncertainty**; and Max Born, with new ideas on waves and quantum mechanics. Even so, Einstein remained the most important scientist of his time.

The theories of Danish physicist Niels Bohr (1885-1962) led to a better understanding of atoms. He suggested that electons move in certain orbits, or "shells."

Einstein was dismayed at the rise of the Nazi party in Germany and their growing displays of military power.

Einstein's scientific work and his views on politics and peace made him a world-famous figure. Crowds gathered to cheer him at this parade in New York, in the 1920s.

Politics and religion

Einstein had been appointed director of the Kaiser Wilhelm Institute in Berlin in 1913. But he often clashed with other scientists in Germany, where anti-Jewish feelings ran high (see panel opposite).

After the defeat of Germany in the First World War, German scientists were unwelcome at many scientific meetings. But Einstein was a well-known supporter of peace and a Jew. So he was accepted as an ambassador for German science.

In 1921 Einstein was awarded the **Nobel Prize** for physics. But this was not for relativity. It was for his less important work on the photoelectric effect. Many people suspected that this strange reasoning was due to pressure from anti-Jewish scientists.

In 1919, Einstein and Mileva divorced. He then went on to marry his cousin Elsa. This photograph of them was taken on a visit to Madrid.

From Germany to America

During the 1920s, Einstein continued to speak out against Germany's political and military aims. When Adolf Hitler and the Nazis came to power in 1933, Einstein was in the United States. Recognizing that his politics and religion would put him in danger, he did not return to Germany. He resigned his post in Berlin and took up a similar one at the Institute of Advanced Study in Princeton, New Jersey. Many other scientists also left Germany at this time, especially physicists and Jews.

Einstein was based at Princeton for the rest of his life. As a person he was shy, retiring, and kind. He did not use his fame to seek great power or wealth. Instead, he lived a quiet life and enjoyed music and sailing.

Einstein's house in Princeton, New Jersey. The town was his adopted home for 22 years.

Adolf Hitler speaks to Nazi supporters. Hitler's troops invaded Poland in 1939, leading to war in Europe.

A great loss

During his later years, Einstein was still active in politics and science. In the 1950s, he protested against the massive investigation and persecution of people suspected of links with **communists** and so-called **un-American activities**. He also campaigned for an end to all nuclear weapons. This was despite his involvement in urging the U.S. government to build the first atom bomb during the Second World War (see panel).

Even in his late fifties, Einstein was producing scientific articles. By this time, he was no longer working at the heart of the scientific community. Yet when he died in Princeton in 1955, the world knew that it had lost one of the greatest scientific minds of all time.

The atom bomb

When the Second World War broke out in 1939, Einstein was persuaded to write a letter to President Franklin D. Roosevelt (above), urging the start of a project to develop an **atom bomb**. Many other scientists did the same. They knew the Germans had discovered the enormous amounts of energy released by splitting atoms. If they could harness this power, they might be able to build atomic weapons.

As a result of this effort, the U.S. built atomic bombs first, dropping two on Japan in 1945. This hastened the end of the Second World War.

President Einstein?

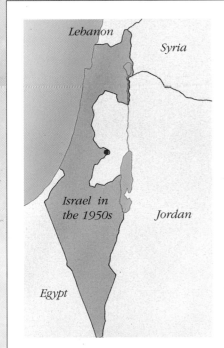

Einstein was a keen supporter of the movement to establish an independent Jewish homeland in the Middle East. This happened in 1948 with the creation of the state of Israel. In 1952, Einstein was offered the position of president of Israel, but he said "no."

The Israeli flag

Discoveries in space

In the past few decades astronomers have begun to discover amazing objects far away in space, such as quasars, pulsars, and black holes. In these situations, the force of gravity is enormous – that is, space-time is extremely curved. General relativity is the basic idea behind all this research. It was also used to develop the idea of the Big Bang, which explains how the universe came into existence.

Chapter Seven

Einstein in Perspective

Today, the theories of relativity are central to science. But they have had different histories.

Special relativity was accepted in a few years. It was in the mainstream of scientific events, and it answered questions that scientists were asking. And it had many uses in the main areas of research being carried out at that time, such as nuclear physics and quantum mechanics.

Today, it is an everyday tool for physicists working on the makeup of matter and the forces that bind it together.

On the grand scale

General relativity applies on a much larger scale to stars and galaxies in deep space. It took longer to be accepted because it did not seem to have many practical uses. Einstein used it to explain the underlying order and simplicity of the universe.

It was not until the 1960s that giant **particle accelerators** and other equipment became more powerful so that parts of the theory could be tested.

Einstein's achievements are remembered in many ways, from medals and plaques to prizes and place names.

ALBERT EINSTEIN 1879-1955

R HUGUENIN

$$E = mc^2$$

Continuing progress

In his later years, Einstein continued to search for a theory that would bring together gravity, electromagnetism, and other kinds of forces and energy in one set of mathematical equations. It was part of his quest to discover the basic way in which the universe worked.

Scientists today are still carrying on these lines of research, trying to create one theory that connects, or unifies, everything. This is called the **grand unification theory.** It has to include the exciting discoveries that continue to be made each year. The continuing hope is to achieve Einstein's dream – a "theory of everything" that explains our universe and everything in it.

Remembered by name

A chemical **element** (basic substance) has been named in honor of Einstein. It is a radioactive metal called einsteinium. It has the symbol Es and the number 99 in the table of elements. Einsteinium does not occur naturally. It is formed in nuclear explosions. Almost instantly, it changes and "decays" into subatomic particles.

The World in Einstein's Time

	1879-1900	1901-1925
Science	1879 Einstein is born 1883 The last quagga, a relative of the horse and the zebra, dies in Amsterdam Zoo 1885 Louis Pasteur successfully tests a vaccine against rabies	1905 Einstein publishes his Theory of Special Relativity 1915 Einstein publishes his Theory of General Relativity
Exploration	1877 Asaoh Hall discovers Mars's two moons, Phobos and Deimos 1881 Henry Stanley founds what is now the town of Kinshasa in Zaire	1912 Robert Falcon Scott dies after reaching the South Pole and finding that the explorer Roald Amundsen got there first 1919 John Alcock and Arthur Brown make the first nonstop flight across the Atlantic Ocean
Politics	1877 Queen Victoria becomes Empress of India 1880s The Third Republic gains firm control in France 1899 The Boer War begins in Africa	1914 First World War begins 1918 First World War ends 1920 Prohibition era begins in the U.S. This means that drinking alcohol is now against the law
Art	1877 Anna Sewell's best-selling children's story *Black Beauty* is first published 1880 Pyotr Tchaikovsky composes the *1812 Overture*	1907 Exhibition of Cubist paintings by Picasso and Braque opens in Paris 1920s Jazz emerges in the U.S., with players such as Louis Armstrong, Duke Ellington, and Count Basie

1926-1950	1951-1975
1926 John Logie Baird demonstrates his mechanical disc television system	**1953** The structure of DNA (the "molecule of life") and the genetic code, is worked out by James Watson and Francis Crick
1945 The Nobel Prize for Physiology, or medicine, is awarded to Alexander Fleming, Ernst Chain, and Howard Florey for their work on penicillin	**1955** Einstein dies
	1958 The first nuclear power station is opened in the US
1927 Charles Lindbergh makes the first nonstop solo flight across the Atlantic Ocean	**1953** Edmund Hillary and Tenzing Norgay are the first people to reach the summit of Mount Everest
1928 Richard Byrd sets up base on Antarctica and flies over the South Pole, beginning the first of five expeditions to map the continent	**1961** Yuri Gagarin orbits the Earth in *Vostok 1*. He is the first person in Space
	1969 Neil Armstrong becomes the first person to set foot on the Moon
1929 The "crash" on the Wall Street stock market in the U.S. causes financial depression all over the world	**1963** President John F. Kennedy is assassinated
	1966 The Cultural Revolution begins in China
1939 Second World War begins	
1945 Second World War ends	
1926 The first film with sound is made. Called *The Jazz Singer*, it stars Al Jolson	**1962** The pop group The Beatles release their first record
1949 Stephen King, one of today's best-selling authors, is born	**1962** The famous film star Marilyn Monroe dies at the age of 36

Glossary

atom: the smallest part of a substance, far too tiny to see under the most powerful light microscope. Atoms can be split into smaller particles, such as *electrons* and neutrons, but these no longer have the physical and chemical features of the original substance (see also *element*).

atom bomb: a bomb which explodes when two nuclei (see *nucleus*) are forced together by a smaller, trigger explosion. The resulting reaction releases huge amounts of radioactive energy (*radioactivity*), creating enormous amounts of damage. The first atom bombs were dropped on Japanese cities in 1945, during the Second World War. These were the world's first *nuclear* weapons.

communists: supporters of communism, a belief that people should work together for the good of their community and not to make money for themselves. In return, the community will give them food, housing, and healthcare.

constant: an amount (written as a number) that never changes. It is always the same.

electron: a type of *subatomic particle* which has a negative charge and is outside the *nucleus* of an atom.

electromagnetic waves: waves of *radiation* which create both electrical and magnetic fields (see also *electromagnetism*).

electromagnetism: when an electric current flows along a conductor (such as a piece of wire) causing the conductor to act like a magnet.

element: a single, pure substance, such as iron or carbon. All the *atoms* of an element are the same as each other and different from atoms of other elements.

equation: a mathematical or chemical "sum" with an equals sign (=) in it, where the two sides balance or are equal.

frequency: for waves such as light and radio, the number of waves passing a particular point in a certain time.

grand unification theory: a belief that it must be possible to describe all the properties and workings of the universe in just one set of *equations*. No one has been able to write such equations so far.

gravity: the attraction or pulling force between one object and another. It is one of the fundamental forces of nature, and all objects possess it. But it is usually used to describe the vast gravitational attraction exerted by the Earth that pulls smaller objects towards its center. Earth's gravity pulls you to the ground when you jump into the air.

mass: in everyday terms, the amount of matter in an object. The scientific definition involves the object's resistance to acceleration. Mass is different from weight, which depends on the gravitational force acting on the object (see *gravity*). An astronaut has the same mass on the Moon and on the Earth, but his weight differs.

molecule: the smallest part of a substance that usually exists on its own and still keeps the chemical and physical features of that substance.

Nobel: the name of prizes awarded each year for great achievements in physics, chemistry, physiology or medicine, economics, literature, and peace. They are named after Alfred Nobel (1833-1896), the Swedish chemist and manufacturer. The fortune made from his invention, dynamite, provides money for the prizes.

nuclear: having to do with the *nucleus*, which is the central part of an *atom*. Nuclear energy gives off *radiation.*

nucleus (plural **nuclei**): the cluster of *subatomic particles*, called protons and neutrons, in the middle of an *atom.*

particle accelerator: a machine in which particles, including those smaller than *atoms*, can be fired at each other at high speed.

physical sciences: also known as physics, these branches of science concentrate on the study of matter and energy and the relationship between them. Modern physics includes the study of *nuclear* energy.

physicist: a scientist who studies the *physical sciences.*

principle of uncertainty: the belief that time and energy or position and speed cannot all be accurately measured at the same time.

quantum physics: a branch of *physical science* based on the proposal that energy comes in tiny "packets" rather than a continuous stream.

radiation: in general, giving out ("radiating") energy in the form of rays, waves or particles. Light rays and radio waves are forms of radiation.

radioactivity: when unstable *atoms* break up and give off certain rays or particles, which can harm living things.

spectrum: the colors of the rainbow, from red to violet, that make up white light.

subatomic particles: particles that are even smaller than *atoms*. Three main types of subatomic particles make up atoms: protons and neutrons in the center or *nucleus,* and *electrons* whizzing around the nucleus.

un-American activities: activities of people accused of being *communists* and working against the interests of the U.S. in the 1950s. Claims of such activities were later found to be exaggerated or untrue.

vacuum: nothingness, a place where there is nothing, not even air. Most of space is a vacuum, but perfect vacuums, which contain absolutely nothing, are quite rare.

Index

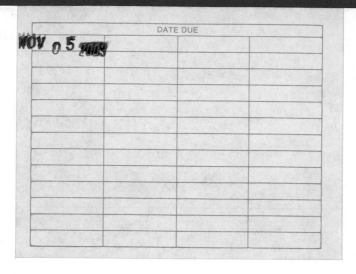

DATE DUE			
NOV 0 5 2003			